PRIMARY CRULLERS

A Robotman Book

JIM MEDDICK

Andrews McMeel
Publishing®

Kansas City • Sydney • London

Andrews McMeel Publishing, LLC
an Andrews McMeel Universal company
1130 Walnut Street, Kansas City, Missouri 64106

www.andrewsmcmeel.com

ISBN: 978-0-8362-3662-0

Library of Congress Control Number: 9771633

Robotman may be viewed at:
www.gocomics.com

7

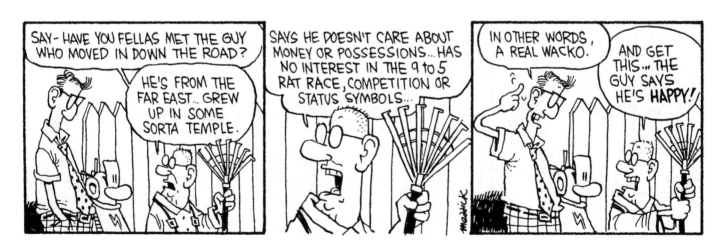

9

14

23

UH-OH. THAT LADY STARTED PUTTING HER GROCERY ITEMS ON THE CONVEYOR BELT BEFORE I COULD PUT DOWN THE "LITTLE WHITE SEPARATOR BAR"...

SHOULD I PUT THE BAR DOWN NOW? OR DOES THAT MAKE ME LOOK UPTIGHT... LIKE I'M WORRIED SHE'S PUTTING HER ITEMS TOO CLOSE TO MINE?

IS IT A COURTESY TO PUT THE BAR DOWN? OR IS IT AN INSULT?

I KNOW. I'LL LEAVE IT UP TO HER. IF SHE WANTS THE BAR, SHE CAN PUT IT DOWN... IF NOT, THAT'S OK TOO!

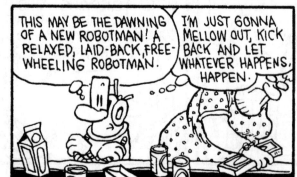

THIS MAY BE THE DAWNING OF A NEW ROBOTMAN! A RELAXED, LAID-BACK, FREE-WHEELING ROBOTMAN.

I'M JUST GONNA MELLOW OUT, KICK BACK AND LET WHATEVER HAPPENS, HAPPEN.

"JUMBO-PACK - GRADE A FANCY PRUNES."

I DON'T WANT TO TALK ABOUT IT.

25

BY NOW YOU'RE PROBABLY ALL FAMILIAR WITH THOSE AMAZING 3-D IMAGES THAT "MAGICALLY" APPEAR OUT OF SEEMINGLY RANDOM DESIGNS.

meddick

WELL AS A LITTLE TREAT FOR OUR READERS, I'VE CREATED ONE MYSELF!

STARE AT THE PANEL BELOW AND GRADUALLY A NAKED 3-D PORTRAIT OF CLAUDIA SCHIFFER PLAYING VOLLEYBALL WILL APPEAR!

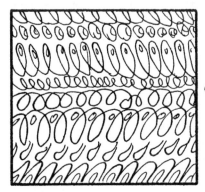

HAVE PATIENCE NOW... IT TAKES AWHILE...

UM... I DON'T THINK YOU DID THIS RIGHT.

I CAN SEE IT FROM HERE! JUST KEEP TRYING!

MY EYES ARE HURTING!

HOLD IT UP TO YOUR NOSE!

Y'KNOW - IT JUST OCCURRED TO ME - YOU PROBABLY SEE NAKED IMAGES OF CLAUDIA SCHIFFER WHEREVER YOU LOOK!

NO, BUT NOW THAT YOU MENTION IT...

...I CAN SORT OF MAKE OUT A TOPLESS IMAGE OF CINDY CRAWFORD IN THIS "MARMADUKE" PANEL.

CRUMPLE CRUMPLE

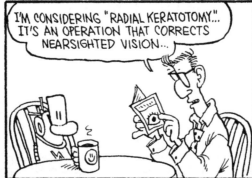

31

OH MY...THE ELEVATOR'S STUCK AND THE ALARM DOESN'T SEEM TO WORK...

WELL, WELL, WELL...THIS SHOULD BE INTERESTING TO SEE WHO CRACKS FIRST...

I DON'T THINK IT'LL BE THE GUY IN THE SWEATSHIRT...HE LOOKS TOUGH... POSSIBLY A 'NAM VET...PROBABLY BEEN IN A BAMBOO CAGE TIGHTER'N THIS...

THE WOMAN?...NO WAY...THAT WOULD BE POLITICALLY INCORRECT...

I SAY SHORTY'S THE WEAK LINK. HE'S SHOWIN' ALL THE SIGNS...FIDGETING... LOOKIN' AROUND...YEP...HE'S GONNA FOLD LIKE AN ORIGAMI SWAN...

HEY...LISTEN...SUDDENLY IT GOT REAL QUIET...

WHA?...WHAT HAPPENED TO THE MUZAK?!...WHAT'S GOING ON?! WE'RE ALL GONNA DIE! DIE! DIE!

HOLD A COMB IN HIS MOUTH SO HE DOESN'T SWALLOW HIS TONGUE! I'LL CLIMB THROUGH THE EMERGENCY PANEL, SHINNING UP THE CABLES AND GET HELP!

MOMMY! MOMMY!

HEY, SORRY I'M LATE, BUT ON MY WAY HERE I DECIDED TO STOP AT L'HOMME DE FAD AND BUY A NEW HAT...

THE SALESMAN SHOWED ME THIS REALLY HIP, CUTTING-EDGE DESIGN OUT OF MILAN. IT COST A FORTUNE AND IT'S NON-REFUNDABLE, BUT HEY, YOU ONLY GO AROUND ONCE!

WHAT D'YOU GUYS THINK?

IT'S WILD.

YEAH. REALLY COOL.

YOU HAVEN'T SAID ANYTHING. WHAT DO YOU THINK?

YOU KNOW THAT STORY, "THE EMPEROR'S NEW CLOTHES"?

YEAH. WHAT ABOUT IT?

THE KING GETS TRICKED INTO WEARING AN IMAGINARY WARDROBE, BUT BECAUSE EVERYONE IS AFRAID OF LOOKING STUPID AND ENRAGING THE KING, THEY ALL COMPLIMENT HIM UNTIL FINALLY A LITTLE KID IS THE ONLY ONE HONEST ENOUGH TO POINT OUT THE KING IS, IN FACT, NAKED...

YEAH YEAH YEAH! WHAT IS THIS? BEDTIME STORY HOUR?! GET TO THE POINT!

THE POINT IS: I REALLY LIKE THE WAY THAT HAT BRINGS OUT THE COLOR OF YOUR EYES...

REALLY? YOU NOTICED THAT TOO?!

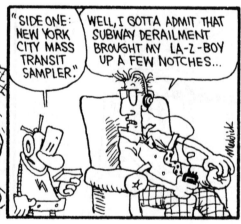

TEN BUCKS T' PLAY. CHANCES OF WINNING ARE 20 QUADRILLION TO ONE, BUT IF YOU SCRATCH OFF THE REAR END OF THE JACK ASS AND SEE A SMILEY FACE, YOU WIN A BILLION DOLLARS AND GET TO LIVE IN THE GOVERNOR'S MANSION WITH "VICTORIA'S SECRET" MODELS AS YOUR SERVANTS...

MONTY ARE YOU NUTS? AT 20 QUADRILLION TO ONE, YOUR ODDS OF WINNING ARE ROUGHLY EQUIVALENT TO THE ODDS OF BILL CLINTON PARACHUTING OUT OF AIR FORCE ONE AND LANDING ON YOUR HEAD IN DRAG...

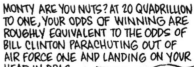

42

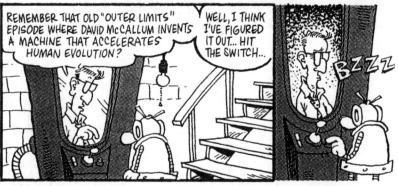

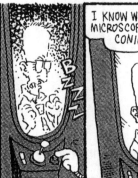

48

WITH THE INTRODUCTION OF *GIGGLES THE BEAR*, ROBOTMAN'S LIFE TURNS AROUND AND READERSHIP REACHES AN ALL-TIME HIGH!

YOU GUYS ARE THE GWEATEST!

Dear Robotman,

I love Giggles! He's totally cute and mentally unchallenging! His jokes are so simple and banal, I always understand them. Thanx, Debbie

Dear Robotman,

After reading today's "Giggles" strip, I cut it out of the paper and cuddled it.

Love,
My inner child

Dear Robotman,

Just one look at "Giggles" and I feel compelled to buy t-shirts, plush toys and thermoses featuring his likeness.
Sincerely,
Ralph Nader

Robotman,

When I saw your new character/product line "Giggles," I felt a peculiar stirring in my loins.

Comic Syndicate Executive

GUESS WHAT?! I'M COOKIN' YOU BWEAKFAST!

NO... NO... YOU DON'T HAVE TO DO THAT...

I KNOW YOU'RE KINDA A GRUMPY GUSS AND YOU'RE NOT USED TO HAVING A CUTE CHARACTER AROUND, SO I THOUGHT I'D DO SUMTHIN' NICE TO WIN YOU OVER...

WHAT'S WONG? LOST YOUR APPETITE?

I'M JUST SORT OF GRAPPLING WITH THE FACT THAT YOU SERVED THE EGGS AND BACON IN THE FORM OF A SMILEY FACE...

NOW WHAT ARE YOU DOING, GIGGLES?

I'M COOKIN' UP SOME OATMEAL FOR GWAMPS...

MY! MY! SUMTHIN'S SMELLIN' MIGHTY SWELL 'ROUND HERE...

KEEP SOAKIN' YOUR FEET, GRAMPS... I'LL BRING YOUR OATS OUT TO THE TUB...

THE PROBLEM WITH CUTE CHARACTERS IS, YOU GIVE 'EM AN INCH AND THEY TAKE A MILE...

WHAT'S REALLY SCARY IS, I DON'T KNOW WHO THE *G#% THAT OLD MAN IS OR HOW HE GOT IN HERE...

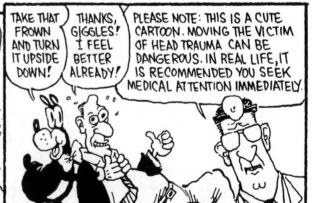

58

WANT SOME?

I'M STILL WORKING ON MY CAPPUCCINO...

SO...UM...I HAVEN'T SEEN YOU AROUND MUCH LATELY...I GUESS YOU'RE PRETTY SERIOUS ABOUT THIS NEW WOMAN YOU'RE DATING...

YEAH, I GUESS SO...

SO, HAS THE "M" WORD COME UP YET?

NO, BUT THE OTHER "M" WORD HAS...

YOU MEAN...?

YEAH, "MOVING IN"...BUT I DON'T KNOW...MAYBE SHE'S RIGHT— MAYBE I'M JUST AFRAID OF COMMITMENT, BUT...I DON'T KNOW...

LIKE EVERY TIME I THINK ABOUT IT, IT SOUNDS OK...BUT THEN THERE'S A LITTLE VOICE INSIDE THAT...WELL...MAKES ME UNSURE...

LIKE EVEN RIGHT NOW I CAN HEAR THE VOICE... IT'S SAYING...IT'S SAYING...

"UPTOWN GIRL...SHE'S BEEN LIVIN' IN HER UPTOWN WORLD..."

THAT'S YOUR WALKMAN.

OH YEAH, RIGHT...LET ME JUST TURN THIS DOWN...

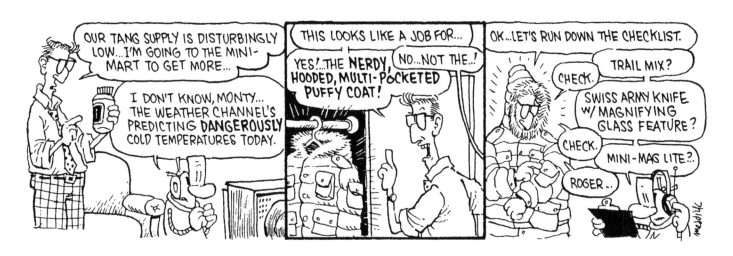

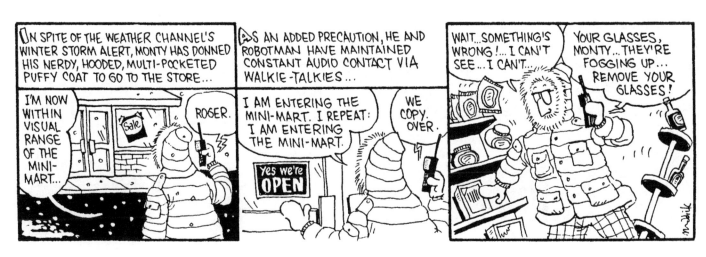

"CHER"

68

MR. MONTAHUE, MEET MR. OTIS...WE BELIEVE HE MAY BE ABLE TO VERIFY YOUR ALIEN ABDUCTION WITH HIS EYEWITNESS ACCOUNT...

I WAS IN THE BACK LOT OF THE LIQ-R-MART AFTER PURCHASIN' A FLASK OF WHITE HORSE WHEN I LOOKED UP IN TH' SKY AND SAW A GLOWIN' YELLOWISH OBJECT HOVERIN' THERE...

...THEN I RUBBED MY EYES... BUT IT WAS STILL THERE!

THEN I RUBBED MY EYES AGAIN AND REALIZED IT WAS A SUNOCO SIGN. BUT BEHIND IT... I'M PRETTY SURE I SAW A UFO. THEN I FELL ASLEEP IN A PUDDLE.

FINALLY, I'M VINDICATED!

FACE IT, MULDER, THIS GUY'S STORY IS THE FLIMSIEST X-FILE OF ALL...MAYBE HE'S JUST A PARANOID GOOFBALL WITH AN OVERACTIVE IMAGINATION.

NO! NO, THAT'S JUST WHAT THE ALIENS WANT US TO THINK!

THAT'S WHY THERE'S NO SOLID EVIDENCE, NO EYEWITNESSES, NO PLAUSIBILITY TO ANYTHING HE SAYS! IT'S ALL A CLEVER PLOT TO DISCREDIT...

OK. CHECK OFF THE "PARANOID GOOFBALL" BOX AND LET'S CALL IT A DAY...

MONEY. MONEY. SEX. SEX. EVERYTHING'S ABOUT MONEY OR SEX. THAT'S ALL THESE ADS ARE ABOUT...

BUT Y'KNOW WHAT?... I DON'T BELIEVE THOSE ARE THE IMPORTANT THINGS IN LIFE... I BELIEVE THE ONLY REALLY IMPORTANT THING IN LIFE IS FRIENDSHIP...

YEAH. IT'S TOO BAD YOU DON'T REALLY HAVE ANY FRIENDS...

DO YOU THINK IF I HAD A COOL CAR PEOPLE MIGHT LIKE ME MORE?...

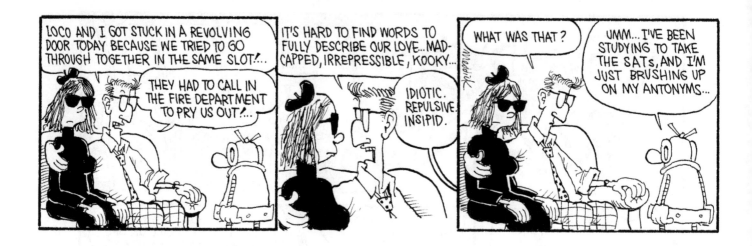

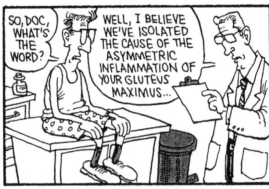

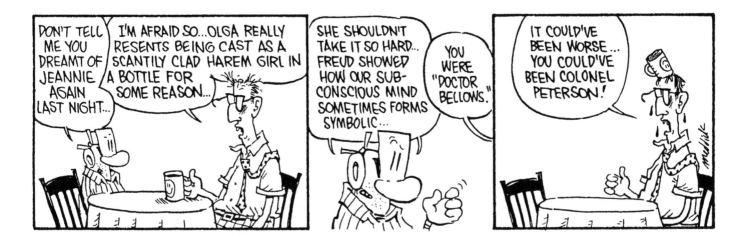

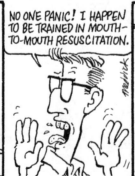

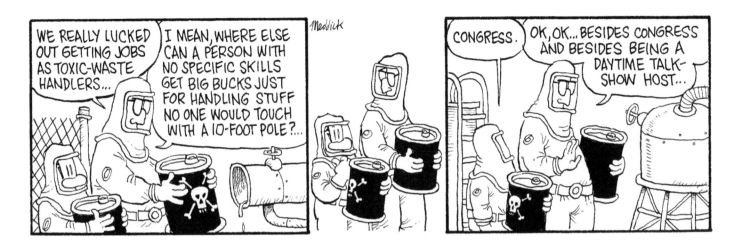

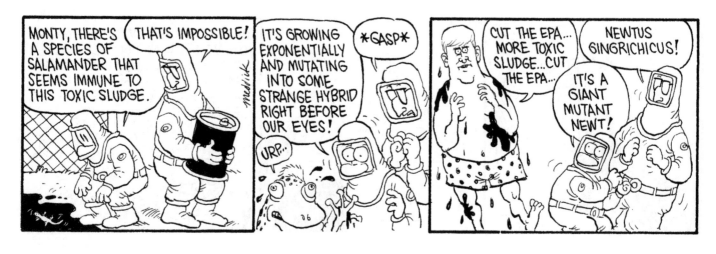

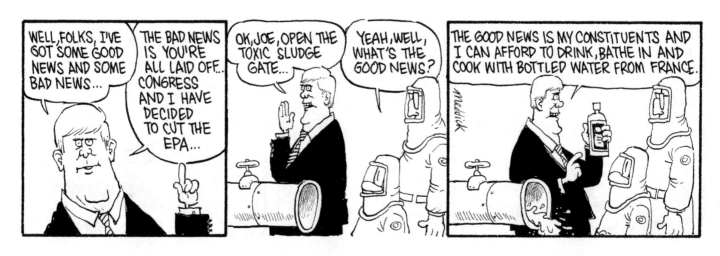

92

I NEVER KNEW YOU WERE INTERESTED IN MODERN ART...

I'M NOT. BUT THIS IS AN EXHIBIT OF MY EX-GIRLFRIEND'S ART...

CHECK THIS OUT...IT'S A BUNCH OF PIGS IN CLOWN COSTUMES SUCKING PACIFIERS AND WALLOWING IN MUD...

AND IT'S ENTITLED SIMPLY "MEN"...

THAT ONE WAS INSPIRED BY OUR RELATIONSHIP.

LOCO! HI!

NOW THAT SHE MENTIONS IT, THERE IS A RESEMBLANCE BETWEEN YOU AND THE ONE WITH THE 666 ON ITS FOREHEAD.

LOCO, I DON'T GET THIS. YOU GLUED STEEL WOOL ONTO A SALTINE BOX?

THAT'S NOT JUST STEEL WOOL ON A SALTINE BOX.

THAT IS A MONUMENT TO MY ANGUISHED SOUL, THE DEATH OF HOPE AND THE INEVITABLE MARCH TOWARD OBLIVION...

WOW. THAT BROUGHT TEARS TO MY EYES. EITHER THAT OR I GOT SOME STEEL WOOL IN MY EYE.

JUST THINKING ABOUT IT, I FIND IT DIFFICULT TO FINISH MY DOUBLE MOCHA CAPPUCCINO.

IT'S...LIKE...UM... NEO-RETRO...UM, MODERNISM... BUT NOT REALLY.

LOCO, YOU AND YOUR ARTIST FRIENDS TALK IN A VAGUE, SPACEY WAY...

IS THAT BECAUSE YOU'RE GENIUSES TALKING ABOUT THINGS TOO COMPLEX FOR WORDS?...OR BECAUSE YOU'RE MORONS?

OH, WOW... IT'S LIKE A MULTIPLE CHOICE TEST.

I TOOK A MULTIPLE CHOICE TEST ONCE. I CHECKED "ALL OF THE ABOVE"..."NONE OF THE ABOVE"! THEN I SET THE TEST ON FIRE...

TAMMY, YOUR STYLIST, IS A FRESH-MAN HERE AT THE HAIRCARE TRAINING INSTITUTE.

HI, TAMMY.

TAMMY...UM...TAMMY...WHAT'RE YOU DOING? DIDN'T YOU READ LAST NIGHT'S ASSIGNMENT ON SYMMETRY?

BZZZZZ

I RILLY MEANT TO...I RILLY DID...BUT MY BOYFRIEND TODD HAD RILLY EXCELLENT TICKETS TO SEE BON JOVI...

DON'T WORRY, MR. MONTAHUE...I'VE ASKED MARCO, OUR MOST ADVANCED TRAINEE, TO FIX TAMMY'S MISTAKES.

LAST NIGHT MARCO WAS INSPIRED BY A NATIONAL GEOGRAPHIC SPECIAL ON AN OBSCURE AMAZONIAN TRIBE!

THERE, MARCO IS FINISHED!

OK. SO IF SOMEONE ASKS, I SHOULD TELL THEM THIS IS THE AMAZONIAN-TRIBE LOOK.

NO, NO. IT WAS THE WAY THEY DEPICTED THEIR MONKEY GOD.

OK...THE HAIRCARE TRAINING INSTITUTE ISN'T PERFECT, BUT THE HAIRCUTS ARE FREE!

AT 15 BUCKS A MONTH, THAT SAVES YOU 180 BUCKS A YEAR!

TAP TAP TAP

AND MIRRORS...I WON'T WANT TO BUY MIRRORS LOOKING LIKE THIS...

I'LL THROW IN AN EXTRA...UM...25 BUCKS.

TAP TAP TAP

OH...AND DATES. I WON'T BE DATING AS MUCH AS LAST YEAR...

OK...$8.75 AT DENNY'S...$3.50 AT BLOCKBUSTER. I'LL START TALLYING...

TAP TAP TAP TAP

101

TO CREATE AN EFFECTIVE ROBOT WARRIOR, I DEVELOPED A HIGHLY SOPHISTICATED COMPUTER BRAIN.

BUT ONCE FITTED WITH THIS BRAIN, THE ROBOT LOSES ALL DESIRE TO MAIM AND DESTROY. IT BECOMES A PBS-WATCHING, VEGETARIAN WUSSY...

ALTHOUGH IT DOES OCCASIONALLY ACQUIRE THE URGE TO GIVE JESSE HELMS A NOOGIE...

DR. MONTAHUE'S PROJECT WAS FAILING. ALL HIS ROBOT WARRIORS WERE PACIFISTS.

THAT'S WHERE BRUCE COMES IN...

BRUCE... ROBOTMAN'S EVIL TWIN!

IN A DESPERATE MOVE TO CREATE A A MEANER ROBOT, MONTAHUE TRIED IMPLANTING THE PERSONALITY OF AN IRS EMPLOYEE INTO ONE OF THE ROBOT PROTOTYPES...

THE EXPERIMENT BACKFIRED. NOT ONLY DID THE ROBOT BECOME INSANELY EVIL, BUT MONTAHUE ENDED UP GETTING AUDITED FOR A DUBIOUS HOME OFFICE...

AH HA HA HA!

NO! NOOO!

MULDER, THERE'RE STILL A LOT OF UNANSWERED QUESTIONS...

LIKE WHY DOES ROBOTMAN THINK HE'S AN ALIEN?

AND WHAT ABOUT THE FAMILY HE USED TO LIVE WITH?

THAT'S ALL EXPLAINED ON THE SECOND VIDEOCASSETTE.

OH, NO. DON'T TELL ME THIS IS A "TO BE CONTINUED" CLIFF HANGER.

YEP... WE'VE EVEN GOT A SHADOWY BACKGROUND CHARACTER TO MAKE IT EXTRA SUSPENSEFUL!

THE ROBOTMAN PROJECT PART 2: THE COVERUP

BE KIND, REWIND.

TO BE CONTINUED!

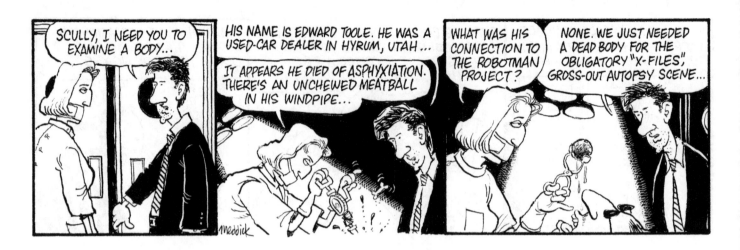

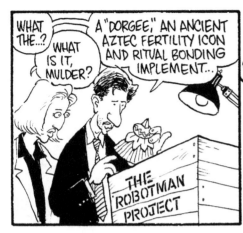

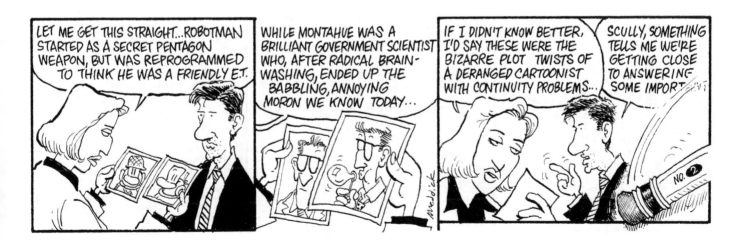

114

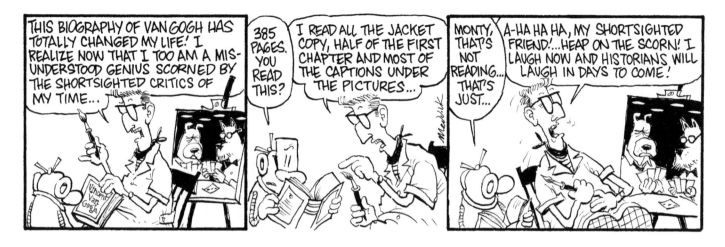

117

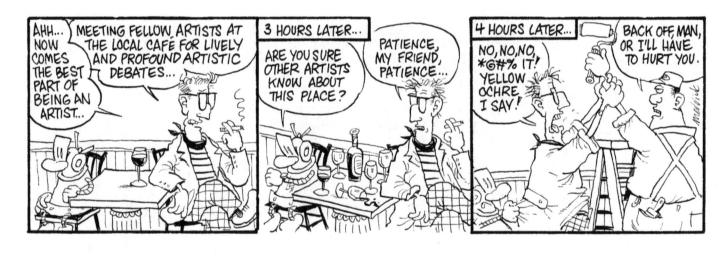

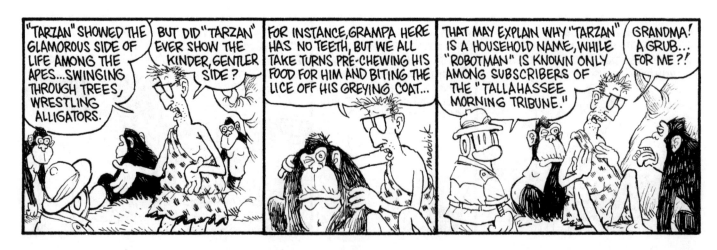

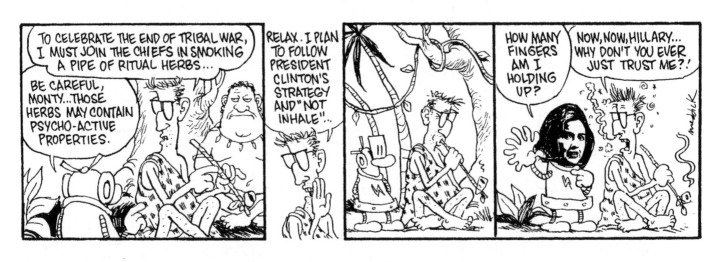

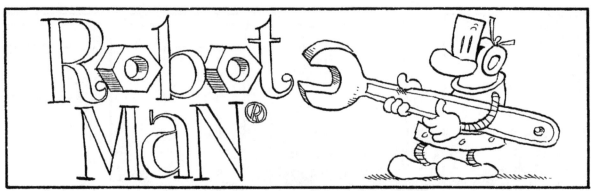